ATLANTIS

ATLANTIS

BY MAUREEN HUNTER

Micheline Steinberg Playwrights
409 Triumph House
187-191 Regent Street
London W1R 7WF
Tel: 020 7287 4383
Fax: 020 7287 4384
Email: steinplays@aol.com

Atlantis
first published 1997 by
Scirocco Drama
An imprint of J. Gordon Shillingford Publishing Inc.
© 1996 Maureen Hunter

Scirocco Drama Editor: Dave Carley
Cover design by Terry Gallagher/Doowah Design
Author photo by Randy Gibson
Cover artwork: *Minoan Snake Goddess* by Mary Valentine
Printed and bound in Canada

Volcano by Jimmy Buffet, Keith Sykes and H. Dailey.
© Coral Reefer Music/Keith Sykes Music, 1979.
Lyrics reprinted with permission of Gelfand, Rennert & Feldman

Published with the generous assistance of The Canada Council

Canadian Cataloguing in Publication Data

Hunter, Maureen, 1947-
    Atlantis

A play.
ISBN 1-896239-23-4

    I. Title.

PS8565.U5814A85 1997   C812'.54   C97-920055-2
PR9199.3.H86A75 1997

For Ken and Margaret Hunter

Acknowledgements

The first draft of *Atlantis* was written while the author was Playwright-in-Residence at Manitoba Theatre Centre, a position made possible through the assistance of the Manitoba Arts Council. It was given a reading by MTC in November 1994 and by Canadian Stage Company, Toronto, in February 1995 and again in June 1995, while the playwright was a member of that theatre's New Play Creation Group. It was workshopped by MTC in December 1995. The playwright is grateful to the theatres involved and to the following actors: Terri Cherniack, Robert Haley, Stavroula Logothettis, Eric Peterson, Dragana Varagic and Janet Wright.

The playwright would also like to thank the following: Steven Schipper for his ongoing commitment to her work, his faith in *Atlantis* and his inspired direction of the premiere production; Stavroula Logothettis and Eric Peterson for their outstanding performances in the premiere production; Candace Burley for many hours of dramaturgical assistance; Dr. R.D. Gold (University of Winnipeg) for his advice and guidance; Anastasia Cholakis, Doug Evans, Areta Stewart and Mary Valentine for research assistance; and the many friends and relatives who offered criticism and support, especially Martha Brooks, Gary Hunter and Stephanie Kostiuk.

Production Credits

Atlantis premiered at Manitoba Theatre Centre, Winnipeg, in co-production with Theatre Calgary, on February 8, 1996 with the following cast:

BEN .... Eric Peterson
MIRCEA .... Stavroula Logothettis

Directed by Steven Schipper
Set and Costume Design by Brian Perchaluk
Lighting Design by Michael Whitfield
Assistant Lighting Design by Scott Henderson
Assistant Director: Robb Paterson
Stage Manager: Margaret Brook
Assistant Stage Manager: Wanda Bretecher

Special thanks to Dr. Michael Eleff, Dr. Marcia Fleisher, and Dr. Carl Ridd.

Characters

BEN, a Canadian, about 50

MIRCEA, a woman of Santorini, not much younger (MIRCEA is pronounced MIR-*SAY*-A)

Setting

The Greek island of Santorini, 1985.

Production Notes

In this play, the characters *never* interact with or acknowledge one another. Their communion is with the audience. The set should facilitate this communion, suggesting the locale as simply as possible, with a few broad-brush strokes. Similarly, costumes and props should be kept to an absolute minimum. Simplicity is the watchword.

In the original production, the set consisted of a multi-levelled rock, offering a variety of playing areas. On one level, a space with a chair represented Ben's room; on another, Mircea's. Other settings on the island were represented by playing areas elsewhere on the rock. A scrim behind the rock opened gradually to reveal a stylized cliff-face. Until Mircea's final words at the end of Act Two, neither actor left the stage.

The spacing used in the text represents the playwright's attempt to convey the rhythm of the speeches as they came to her. Adherence to this rhythm should be respectful but not rigid.

Note: The minotaur is usually described as a creature with a man's body and a bull's tail, hoofs and head. In this play, the playwright has chosen to combine the physical characteristics of man and bull in a somewhat different manner.

Maureen Hunter

Maureen Hunter is a Winnipeg playwright whose work has attracted international attention. She is the author of six full-length plays, including *Transit of Venus*, which premiered at Manitoba Theatre Centre in November 1992 and has since been produced across Canada, and in Britain by the Royal Shakespeare Company and by BBC Radio. Following its Toronto production in 1995, *Transit* was nominated for a Dora Mavor Moore Award for Outstanding New Play. Other plays include *Beautiful Lake Winnipeg* and *Footprints on the Moon*, which was nominated for the 1988 Governor General's Award for Drama.

Man desires to recover the active presence of the gods;
he also desires to live in the world as it came
from the Creator's hands, fresh, pure, and strong…
In Christian terms, it could be called a nostalgia for paradise.

Mircea Eliade, *The Sacred and the Profane*

ACT ONE

BEN: Listen. Can you hear that? It falls across you like a blanket, like a benediction, if you listen, if you

Learn to listen.

There it is again; hear it?

Silence.

In that silence lies more truth than in any words.

In language as we use it, there's not much truth. There's truth here *(Indicates the chest.)* and here *(In dicates the stomach.)*. Other places. On the face perhaps. But on the tongue?

That's why I like to carve. I like the notion of creating things I know are honest.

When I've finished a carving, I give it away. I walk out of my room in Akrotiri, onto the road that winds down to the dig, and I give my carving to anyone I meet. At first this caused a little consternation: people don't expect to be given things. By a mute Canadian. I don't speak to them, you see, I never say a word. I simply hand across the carving. Then I walk away.

In homes all over Santorini, now, you'll find my carvings. Do you see what I've accomplished? In all those homes there is at least a little honesty.

Just now I'm carving a goddess—a copy of a goddess who was worshipped on this island

Many centuries ago. You may think her bizarre. I
like her. I call her Pasiphae, which was probably
not her name. No one knows her name. She isn't
finished yet, of course, but when she is you'll see
her breasts are bare—it was the fashion of the
time—and in each hand she holds a snake, a writhing snake. Because of the snakes she's thought to be
an earth goddess. No one knows for sure, because

She's silent. And the person who first carved her is
more silent still.

I think of that person, that long dead person, as I
work. He could have been many things: petty, de-
ceitful, weak, cruel. Whatever he was in life, he is
this in death: he is profoundly honest.

The dead, being silent, must be honest.

I have great admiration for the dead.

On Santorini, at the end of the day, I sit at my
window and stare out at the sea. Sometimes I hear
a donkey bray. Sometimes a voice or a fragment of
song wafts up the hillside from the taverna down
below. Sometimes, in the distance, a motorbike
careens around a curve. Mostly there is silence. The
sky, the sea, and silence.

On Santorini, which was once Atlantis, silence falls
like a benediction on my soul.

MIRCEA: I was to have been named Agalia   Agalia means joy. It was my father's mother's name   her father's mother's name and on and on backwards through the generations   always in my father's family there had been an Agalia   spreading joy. Now it would be my turn   it was understood.

My mother wouldn't have it. On the night that I was born she had a dream she said   she dreamt a stranger handed her a stone on which was carved the name Mircea   a name no one had heard of   that meant nothing   wasn't Greek. My father tried to reason with her   begged her   bribed her   tried to shame her   she was adamant. I became Mircea with one stroke she freed me   this is what she always tells me   thanks to me you could be special   I knew you would be special from the moment of conception   this is what she always says.

And I did believe it   I let myself believe it   but just now she started in again   the dream   the stone   the stranger and suddenly I saw the awful truth. Oh it's true she freed me   with one stroke she freed me but from what   the weight of custom   or the promise of joy.

BEN: When I came here, to this island, I was empty,
            empty. Hollow as a drum. Little things got me
            through. The handle on the door leading to my
            room; something about the shape of it. The table
            under the window: solid, plain, a little scarred. The
            weight of my spoon. A simple thing like that! The
            weight of an ordinary spoon. The way my window
            framed the sea. The silence.

            I don't know when it was—much later—I began to
            pick up scraps of wood. In the ditches, by the road-
            side: if I kept my eyes to the ground I'd often find
            them. They puzzled me, in some vague way. I'd set
            them on the window-sill when I got home. I'd
            study them.

            Then one day, in a shop in Oia, I saw a set of tools
            for carving wood. I'd never owned such things, I'd
            never even held them in my hand. I found I liked
            the weight of them, the shape, the feel. The cool
            hard promise of the blades.

            I didn't buy them right away. I came back to my
            room, examined all my scraps again. I saw them
            with a different eye. I saw that in each scrap of
            wood a form was growing. A funny thing to say,
            and yet it's true. There was a form inside it, waiting
            to get out.

            I bought the tools. I set to work.

            From the first piece of wood a cat emerged, a poor
            misshapen cat. Much too odd to give away. I
            named him Minos. He sits always just inside my
            door. I like to tease him. Rest, I tell him, you'll
            exhaust yourself. Or: Eat, you'll waste away.

            He doesn't answer. He may be ugly but he's
            honest.

MIRCEA:

Sometimes I hate her. I know it's wrong to say it God forgive me but I do   the way she watches me the eyes like beads the sagging skin   the hands misshapen clinging clinging   all her life a lamentation all her miseries spread out around her to consider day by day. I take such trouble with her meals she seldom eats them   only picks at them a little her mouth is occupied you see   the moans the groans the sighs   how can you get a fork in there with all that going on   it is a problem.

She tells me that she loves me   I suppose she does   I know she loved my father   fell to pieces when she lost him   so I understand I wouldn't know   he drowned when I was three. She says he drowned.

When I was small I'd dream about him   I'd be walking in the village turn a corner then I'd see him he would know me right away. And he'd take me on his knee   I remember every detail   his hands so tanned   the black hairs at his wrist   his shirt too white it hurt my eyes I had to close them which I didn't want to do. And he always said Mircea you must learn to swim Mircea   either that or sprout a pair of wings   I think the odds are better with the sea. Now why would he say that I ask you   why.

I think he saw the future   saw it closing in around us   only he was smarter stronger   he got out before it caught him   before the future caught him he had flown.

BEN: There's something about being in exile that makes
                you feel like Ulysses. You're always searching for
                Ithaca

                Even when you think you're not.

                This morning I went as usual to the dig. As usual
                they turned me away. I'm not allowed to work
                there; why, I couldn't say. Because I'm not an ar-
                cheologist? I don't speak Greek?

                I show up every morning, anyway. They grin, and
                shake their heads. They think I'm a little slow.

                They don't know that I'd do anything, any kind of
                labour, just for the chance to move among them, in
                that ancient city, just to watch them

                Brushing the dust from pieces of antiquity. From
                pieces of Atlantis!

                After a while I wandered off towards Perissa.
                Looking for my scraps of wood. I bent to pick one
                up, and suddenly

                Found myself transported back to Lake Margue-
                rite. I don't mean just in memory; I mean I actually
                stood there, on the porch overlooking the lake. In
                the distance that familiar ring of hills. It was Au-
                gust, a little after dawn: the sun hovered just above
                the graveyard. There was a breeze rising from the
                lake; it set the willows trembling. On the breeze the
                faint enticing smell of new-mown hay.

                It was the smell of hay, I think, that did it. I smelled
                the hay, and then the scene dissolved. I found my-
                self on Santorini, washed in pain.

                I remembered I'm alone. I've lost it all.

MIRCEA: I confess I am by nature quite passionate   I was
             conceived at the end of summer   it was very dry as
             always   the meltemi blew across the island like a
             madness   only if you know these winds these hot
             incessant winds can you begin to understand.

             How they came together to conceive me this is
             something I don't think of   I try not to think of
             my father I can picture but not her   even when I
             strip away the years not her. He was a sailor   I can
             see him in the doorway   dark skin white shirt very
             lean always going out or coming in this is all I can
             remember   a dark shape in the doorway and the
             brightness of the street beyond.

             When I was young my friends would talk about it
                 marriage sex and having babies   the three to-
             gether always like the Holy Trinity. Not me   I
             wanted only one I wanted it but not with any boy
             I knew or else with all of them. As I look back I see
             the signs were there my life would go a certain way
                 no middle ground   no in between   a whore or a
             madonna as my mother said   I don't know which
             is better which is worse this much I know they're
             not as far apart as they might seem.

BEN: I dreamt of it again last night, an island washed in light. A dream I've had since childhood, but last night I saw it for the first time from above, a god's eye view, and understood at last

It was Atlantis. It was this very island that I stand on now. I've dreamt it all my life!

You can't imagine what a shock it was: to recognize the place at last. I felt elated

Then suddenly afraid. It looks so fragile, from that height, and so

Impermanent. It doesn't even seem connected to the earth; it seems afloat. It floats on the sea, this island, like a crown cast down by a god.

In fact it's not an island only but a group of islands—Santorini like an open mouth around the bay. I say the bay: this of course is the caldera, where the mountain stood, before it blew, before it blasted fifty cubic miles of rock into the sky, before the sea poured in

To fill the hole

The gaping monstrous hole

That had been mountain.

My God, when you think about it. What a waterfall that must have been.

MIRCEA: Today in the village a funeral   cicadas singing in
the hot still air   the women keening by the grave
the coffin piled with flowers   I did a thing I've
never done   amazed them all   amazed myself as
well.

The priest droned on   the heat the dust   I felt a little
faint   too many words I thought for such a man
too many words at far too many graves   too many
widows clinging to my hand

And suddenly a goat   Elina's goat broke through
the ring of mourners   snatched a flower from the
coffin stood there munching it as though it were a
feast. A silence fell across us   no one moved   I
heard the widow gasp   she crossed herself   the
goat blinked twice and twitched its tail   that's
when I laughed I couldn't help it   then a child
laughed with me   someone flashed a smile   then
an argument erupted over who should move the
goat   in the time it took to work this out the old
goat wandered off   the priest sighed deeply closed
his prayer book   everyone was thankful   that was
that.

But as we turned to leave the widow clutched my
hand   you'll come to see me won't you   tonight
tomorrow Thursday   I need your help Mircea   I
don't want to be alone I'm so afraid. I knew what
she expected   that I'd say of course I'll be there
and I meant to say it everyone was waiting but the
words the words the words

Would not be formed. It was the thought of all that
listening   all those hours of listening while she
mourned lamented sorrowed   filled my ears with
secrets I don't want to know her secrets   it was
suddenly too much to bear. I stepped back pulled
my hand free   turned and hurried from the church-
yard   left them standing by the graveside   their
mouths agape their eyes astonished   you'd think
the dead had risen   you'd think a figure carved in
stone had turned and walked away.

BEN: I've been a fool.

I just came back from Fira. I go there once in a while, don't ask me why. Because I'm a fool, that's why.

I'd been thinking about my dream—about the strange

Coincidence of finding myself, now, on an island I've dreamt about since I was five. How can this be? I came here on a whim, I thought; pure chance. But did I? Was it?

I went for a walk—still pondering these things—and found myself in Fira, standing on the edge of the caldera. Watching the donkeys labour up and down the face of the cliff. With their precious cargo of tourists. I turned to leave, and there, staring me in the eye

Well, it doesn't matter who it was. Someone I'd rather not have seen. A Canadian who knew me when I

When

He started to speak but I slipped away, I lost myself amongst the throngs of tourists. Then hurried back to Akrotiri. My whole body wet with sweat, my heart pounding like a jackhammer.

I'm a little calmer now. I picked up a bottle of retsina in the village.

Tastes like kerosene, but you get used to it.

MIRCEA: Tonight I knelt for hours in the church   at the feet
                 of the Blessed Virgin   gave her an earful. I didn't
                 mean to do it there was no one else to talk to   who
                 am I to talk to   who am I to turn to when I   when

BEN: *(Sings.)* "I don' know

                I don' know

                I don' know where I'm agonna go when the vol-
                cano blows.

                I don' know

                I don' know

                I don' know where I'm agonna go

                When the volcano..."

MIRCEA: At midnight I went to see the widow   sat with her
                 most of the night   listened to her sorrows   heard
                 her secrets   held her hand. I asked her to remember
                 paradise   we all remember paradise   call it what
                 you like I call it ecstasy   it's the place we've come
                 from   and the place we're going to.

BEN: I got up this morning and started to pack. Brush,
            toothbrush, razor. Socks, shorts. Carving tools.

            Then I glanced at Minos. Turned to stare at the sea.

            Listened to the silence.

            Unpacked.

MIRCEA: We circle from ecstasy to ecstasy   this is what I
believe   the time we spend on earth is like a sigh
nothing more. I say this even on a night like this the
sky ablaze with stars   I didn't say it wasn't beautiful this earth   I only said the time we spend here is
a sigh. Out of ecstasy we come   back to ecstasy we
go   we cling to the memory the hope all through
our lives   sometimes glimpse it in the distance but
it's gone before we can be certain   sometimes try to
grasp it but it slips between our fingers   yet we
know we always know it   we know the thing we're
missing   no one ever has to tell us what it is. This
to me is proof.

BEN: Today I bought a ticket at the kiosk and entered the dig as a tourist. When I stepped inside a cheer went up: I'd finally figured it out.

I sat for hours in the ancient city. Imagined it as it must have been when the island was round and full, a tall volcanic mountain at its centre. Imagined the people moving through the sunlit streets. It wouldn't be so different, I suppose. There'd be pots of basil on the windowsills. Laundry hanging out to dry. Dogs lying prostrate in the heat. Shrines here and there, perhaps to the goddess Pasiphae. Carvings of her, maybe, much like mine

And suddenly I felt a longing so profound

It was like an ache. Can you do that, can you actually

Physically ache? For a time and place you've never known?

MIRCEA: Just now outside the market I turned and saw the
            stranger   coming up the hill towards us from the
            dig his head bowed low as always lost in thought.
            They laugh about it in the village he goes all across
            the island this is what they're always saying from
            one end to the other he sees nothing but his feet.

            I knew I shouldn't do it   not there in front of half
            the village but I did I stood and watched him   I
            could sense a pain a longing I watched him and I
            and I caught my breath.

BEN: I buy a ticket every day now, at the dig. Sit for
                 hours in the ancient city, dreaming. Then I come
                 home and carve Pasiphae.

                 I carve, and carve. The hours slip away on me. But
                 sometimes as I carve I have a sense

                 I don't know how to say it. A sense of something
                 present, a feeling at certain moments that if I were
                 to turn and glance behind, I'd catch a glimpse

                 Of what?

                 Of nothing.

                 No, it's really nothing. It's a feeling; nothing more.

MIRCEA: I watch him every morning from my window   al-
            ways the same   white shirt khaki shorts a hat   his
            head down watching his step his eyes in shadow.
            Often the children run after him   a carving mister
            any carvings   but he doesn't seem to hear or else he
            stops and smiles and looks confused. It's that con-
            fusion that endears him to me   he's so grateful   so
            surprised.

            He must be lonely yet he keeps alone   buys what he
            needs in the village   never stops in the kafenio
            hardly ever speaks   they say his Greek is poor
            perhaps that's why. Once a month he picks up his
            mail   there are never any letters   this to me is
            strange.

            I see him in the evenings at his window staring out
            to sea   staring staring   doesn't he get tired the same
            old sea the same old sky   I've known it all my life a
            glance from time to time will tell you all you need
            to know   and yet he stares and stares. Evangelos
            my cousin when I asked about him only shrugged
                he's a crazy bugger that was all he'd say   a few
            holes in the net you know Mircea   we don't let on
            we notice   we just let him be.

BEN: Something has happened. I can't explain it, something

                Unexpected. At times I don't believe it. After all, I didn't think

                I thought

MIRCEA: He looked at me and something flashed between us you can laugh I know it's true a light a spark something more than words not a question recognition a sudden recognition then he smiled. He smiled you see he knew.

And now he comes with carvings three already hands them to me silently but always in his eyes that look that look you could live on it that look.

BEN: I've never laid eyes on a woman like this, I've never

Known anything like this before. She seems to draw you through her when you look at her. When you dare to look. It happens in a flash, it's like being

Yanked through the eye of a needle, you have a glimpse of something. Then it's gone. And it's all you can do to walk away. It's all you can do to walk.

There's something else I can't explain. Everywhere she goes, the men fall silent. I watched her yesterday, today, on Wednesday, moving through the streets. I watched the way the men behave. The way they want to look at her, but don't. The way their voices drop, and fall away. What is that, is it fear? Or reverence.

She moves through the streets, through the village, and in her wake the conversations stop. Even the old men on their chairs in the shade—even they fall silent. She goes from shop to shop and the boys— young boys, barely ten or twelve—run to open doors for her. Then they blush, fall back. Fall silent.

She lives with her mother—this I've just discovered—in a house I pass each morning on my way down to the dig. It seems remarkable to think I've passed that house a hundred times and didn't know. Now whenever I approach I find my breath quickens. I look for her in the window, in the doorway, and she's often there. We don't speak, or smile. I give her a carving if I have one. Sometimes our fingers touch. I meet her eyes, and once again that strange sensation.

I stumble like a drunk man down the hill.

MIRCEA: These things he carves I wouldn't call them beauti-
            ful   at times grotesque   the bird for instance   it's
            not like any bird I've ever seen but you can feel
            I don't know how to say it   something almost like
            a heartbeat like a living heart inside the wood. I
            want to touch it hold it I'm afraid to   maybe it
            would shudder   shake loose from its slumber
            spread its awkward wings and flutter off to find
            the sky.

BEN: It's remarkable that in the silence that surrounds
                    her, the silence she trails after her, I've managed to
                    learn her name.

                    Mircea. Not a name I've ever heard, Mircea. I find it
                    comes quite readily to mind. Slips smoothly off the
                    tongue. Has a kind of

                    Rhythm. In fact, it has the rhythm of my carving.
                    You carve with a certain rhythm, you see; you have
                    to bring a rhythm to the wood. I say this as though
                    I've always known it. Not so. It's only lately, since
                    I've learned her name, since I've learned to say it

                    As I work

                    That I've come to understand: you can't carve well
                    without it. I look at my cat, my Minos. Poor pitiful
                    Minos! If I'd known then what I know now, if I'd
                    cottoned on to this a little sooner

                    Well. He'd be a handsome bugger, I can tell you
                    that.

MIRCEA: Again that dream I wake to find my feet already on
             the floor. I cross the room and from the window I
             can see it's early barely four   the moon is sinking
             back into the sea   a round dark moon   it tries to
             pull the clouds down with it but they slip away. I
             dress quickly steal out quietly then run along the
             road that leads up to the cliffs. And they are there
             where I have seen them in the past   the shapes I
             call my shadows   there is light around them   in the
             centre of the light they dance   a violent ecstatic
             silent dance. I don't know who they are exactly yet
             they seem familiar   as though I've always known
             them   as though I have a knowledge of them in my
             veins.

             I don't disturb them   I hang back amongst the
             rocks I have no sense of time. But when the sky
             begins to lighten they turn the way they always do
             towards the sea   the cliffs dissolve   I see a gentle
             rolling field   they slowly drift away across the
             field. I walk home easily as though my heels were
             wings   as though my body were transparent   this
             is how it always is. And the dream I had the dream
             that starts it all I find I can't remember   nothing not
             a detail   this to me is strange.

BEN: Last night I couldn't sleep. I was standing at my
                window in the early hours—well before dawn,
                when the island is alive with shadows. And I saw
                her. She was on the road that leads up to the cliffs.
                I know it was her, she's unmistakable. There's no
                one on the island who can move like that. Totally
                sure-footed, even in the dark.

                I think an hour passed; more likely two. And then I
                saw her coming back. She had that loose, that easy,
                careless sort of

                Stride that women get, you know, that women

                Afterwards. That kind of stride.

                Only it's not a lover. It's no lover. I don't know how
                I know that, but I do.

MIRCEA: Yesterday he gave me the goddess   after all the
               little birds the animals the fish suddenly a goddess
                  and it's almost beautiful   the arms extended
               holding snakes   the narrow waist   the breasts
               completely bare   it was the fashion of the time. I
               think of him carving the breasts   with such care he
               carved them   what was he thinking how did he feel
               a man carving a woman's breasts.

               He has a scar below the lip just here   a little scar. I
               want to touch it   yesterday I almost did I almost

BEN: When I give her a carving, now, she folds my hands
              in hers. First, before she takes it. It's only a gesture,
              a motion, before I know it's happened she's drawn
              away and in her hands I see the carving. Magic. No,
              it's only a gesture.

              I don't know why I feel so moved.

MIRCEA: She knows. Don't ask me how   she hardly ever
                 leaves her room   lies there huddled in the shut-
                 tered darkness seldom has a visitor at least while
                 I'm at home and yet she knows   she sat me down
                 this morning   read me the gospel   this will be the
                 end of everything she says   the end of you.

BEN: She becomes, this Mircea

More and more mysterious. Just now, as I approached her house, I noticed one of the villagers
set a basket on the doorstep, filled with bread and
cheese. He made the sign of the cross as he set the
basket down, just as though it were

An offering of some kind.

MIRCEA: Today there came for him a letter. I know because
             Elina told me   with such glee she told me. In a
             feminine hand she said. Why tell me this I said it's
             no concern of mine it's no concern of yours with a
             shrug I said this   walked away. That Elina   Face-
             of-a-Dog they call her   one of God's embarrass-
             ments   when her mother cried out on the birthing
             bed He glanced away   that's why Elina looks the
             way she does everyone knows this.

             At home I counted his carvings   eleven now
             eleven. Not enough.

BEN: I haven't opened it. I can't quite bring myself to
              throw it out. But I haven't opened it. I won't. It's
              finished, all of it, it's

              Finished. It might as well have happened in an-
              other life.

MIRCEA: This afternoon while she's asleep I think about my
             life   this man   why now why not when I was
             younger and why him. He isn't all that handsome
                seems so pensive   sometimes comes with mis-
             matched socks the shoulders stooped a little and
             the silence all that silence   who could love a man
             who never speaks a man a man

             Who'll go away. He will they always do   that's
             what my mother says   they're on the run from
             something or they wouldn't end up here at all   and
             you can see it in the face the mouth the lines around
             the eyes   it's there the thing he's running from   it
             hasn't let go yet.

             If I could I'd put a stop to it   blow out the lamp
             before the curtain catches fire. But then I see him
             climbing up the hill   his hat a shadow on his chest
             his hands so empty and I want them on me   asto
             thaylo can't an empty hand be just an empty hand
             and not a miracle. Oh Mircea what's come over you
             Mircea   you were saving yourself remember   for
             the gods.

BEN: I had pulled myself away from her just now—not
            that I had touched her, I had no carving with me,
            nothing at all to give her, but I find it takes a certain

            Effort of will

            To turn and walk away. I'd done it, I was halfway
            up the hill when something made me hesitate and
            turn. She was standing where I'd left her, staring
            after me, her face

            Her face

            I couldn't stand it. I strode back down the hill to-
            wards her, not knowing what I'd do but when I
            reached her

MIRCEA: He took my face between his hands and kissed me
                 gently on the mouth   I felt his breath across my
                 tongue   across my tongue   such a simple thing
                 and then he pulled away   he turned and climbed
                 back up the hill. I didn't move I was afraid to move
                 afraid to breathe   I noticed I was smiling   what a
                 funny thing to stand there smiling at your shadow
                 in the street.

BEN: I want to carve her.

Lately I can think of nothing else. I can see the finished carving in my mind—every detail, every living line. My fingers ache to do it.

But I can't. She needs an artist's hand, and I'm no artist. No, no, I don't deceive myself in this. I know my limitations.

If I were to carve her, this is what I'd do. She'd be standing (as I often see her) with one hand extended, reaching out towards a passer-by. No, let's be honest here: reaching out to me. And on her face that look I see so often. How can I describe it? A look of something waiting to be born.

Her lips

Her lips are parted, just a little. Her forehead very high and clear. There are a few

Rebellious waves of hair against her face, just at the temples; the rest is tied quite loosely at the neck. It would be a simple thing, a very simple thing

To set it free.

But it's the eyes, the eyes. You'd never get them. And it's the eyes you need.

MIRCEA: Last night we were together. How it happened I
can't say   a mystery   to me a miracle. I couldn't
sleep   and then that dream   I rose   changed
quickly slipped outside   I took the road that leads
up to the cliffs but halfway up I turned and he was
there behind me. He didn't look surprised he
looked as though he knew I'd be there   walked
straight to me   touched my cheek   untied my hair
      undid three buttons pulled my dress below my
shoulders   let it fall. Said one word   Mircea   said
it endlessly Mircea. Put his lips in all the places I'd
been saving for the gods.

BEN:

There are gods at work on this island. You can laugh; I know it's true. They've been here all along—I sensed it, yes, I felt their presence but it's only since Mircea that I

Since

Last night...I was shaken from my sleep. I mean it when I use that word, I choose it carefully. And I was instantly awake, and instantly I knew: she's on that road. She's there, and you must go to her. The thought, you see? The thought already planted.

So I knew I'd see her, it was no surprise, but she

But she

She was surprising all the same.

Last night. I was shaken from my sleep, I tell you; shaken.

MIRCEA: I gaze into the mirror out the window laugh at
             nothing forget the thing I started out to do. I bend
             to pick up something then realize I'm smiling feel
             his lips again the touch so urgent feel his hands his
             thighs his belly   I have to reach for something or
             I'll fall. This is new to me this knowledge   all the
             things the skin remembers   all the memories the
             body holds.

             I hear the bell it's ringing ringing how long has it
             been ringing outside her door I hesitate I take the
             time to cover up my thoughts. And of course she's
             angry she has lost her book her glasses   hates the
             heat the flies the silence must she always be alone.
             For a while I sit beside her with a book   pretend
             I'm reading   I don't fool her though she watches
             me   she knows.

             When she falls asleep I leave her   slip downstairs
             clear up the dishes   plunge my hands in water   in
             a dishpan full of water stand there staring while
             the hours drip away. Is he like this   is he aching
             every part of him alive and throbbing   is he aching
             aching aching for my touch.

BEN:　　　　I came up the hill this afternoon like a man who had suddenly sprouted wings. I mean it when I say this: I didn't walk, I flew.

And all the way up my heart was in turmoil. Would she be waiting for me in her doorway? Would she reach out to me as she has before? But again I had nothing to give her, no carving, no excuse to touch her, to let my fingers graze her fingers, there, in the bright light of day, in full view, in the street. What an act of anarchy that's been, I see this now, what erotic license we have taken with each other: to stand there, in broad daylight, and let our fingers touch.

She wasn't standing in her doorway, she was standing in the street. In a dress the colour of the sea. Her hair tied simply at the neck, tied loosely like an open invitation. With one finger, in my mind as I approached, I pulled the ribbon from her hair and set it free. Wove my fingers through it, lifted it and let it fall, buried my face in it, breathed deeply, breathed it in as though it held the breath of life.

All this in my mind, or so I thought

Until I felt her arms go round me, felt her body shudder, and realized the thing I'd just imagined

I'd just done.

MIRCEA: Of course it's madness   no one has to tell me this
            especially not her   but it's no ordinary madness
            it's the madness of the gods. I think I understand
            them now   they were no fools those gods   once
            they'd had a taste of it they couldn't get enough   I
            don't mean sex I mean intoxication   rapture joy
            infatuation   these things aren't human are they
            they're divine   they make us humans feel that
            we're divine.

            We circle from ecstasy to ecstasy   this I still believe
            but sometimes as we move between these poles we
            step into a beam of light   a stream of shimmering
            light   and in that light we glimpse the place we've
            come from and the place we're going to. We step
            into a stream of light and shimmer with the gods.

BEN: Today we met at Red Beach. It was the first time
            we'd been together since

            The first time.

            She seemed a little shy. We didn't speak. After all,
            her English

            My Greek.

            We lay together in a little cove. What a cautious
            phrase: we lay together. What a pristine, cautious,
            blessedly understated phrase.

            Afterwards, tangled in each other's arms, we fell
            asleep. I dreamed of islands washed in light. Of
            caves, and olive groves, and bees.

            When I woke, she was standing knee-deep in the
            sea. Her hair was loose and wet and shining. She
            wasn't naked but she might as well have been: her
            dress clung to her body, transparent as a revela-
            tion.

            It was hot, and very bright. The sun was playing
            tricks on me. She seemed to shimmer in a stream of
            light. I saw her do a thing no one can do. I saw her
            bend, and dip her hands into that stream of light.
            And gather it in her palms, and turn, and offer it to
            me.

MIRCEA: His eyes take their colour from the sea   when he
            stares at it the colour deepens   it's as though he
            draws the sea in draws it deep. I leave the water's
            edge and walk towards him   he is hungry for me I
            can feel it but he doesn't move he only watches
            leans back on his arms and watches   he likes to
            watch me walk I don't know why. When I kneel in
            front of him he suddenly sits forward   takes my
            hands and turns them over   licks the palms the
            fingers   says I taste of salt and sunlight   says he
            wants me needs me loves me   says he'll worship
            me forever   without words he says this   who
            needs words.

BEN: This morning when I wake I'm conscious suddenly

Of light. The way the light invades my room. Light
on the sea reflected on the walls, the ceiling. Light
in my lap as I sit to read. Light filling my mind,
draining, filling it again. Light draped across my
bed, like a lover, like a

Still, expectant lover. A feeling washes over me

I can't define. I travel in my mind

From Santorini back to Lake Marguerite. I remember the joy I felt there, as a boy—the simple joy of
light on water. It's been a long time, but it seems
that after all

I still know what that is.

MIRCEA: He rises from the bed from loving me and carves.
                 He bends to the wood as he bends to me   arches his
                 back and carves   with such strength such longing
                 such intensity he carves it makes me jealous of the
                 wood. I watch him for a while sometimes for hours
                     eventually I fall asleep. And wake to find him
                 standing by the bed   he stands there burning
                 when I reach for him his skin feels hot   on fire   I
                 smile and draw him down   he bends and arches
                 takes me as he takes the wood. My turn.

BEN: I feel like Picasso. I feel like Rodin. I feel

MIRCEA: Again that dream   I run up to the cliffs and they
are there as always   dancing in a ring of shifting
light. Still no more than shadows but this time they
seem to see me   sense my presence   turn towards
me   I feel a rush of terror then a rising joy. For a
moment I don't understand then suddenly it
comes to me   I know these feelings I have had them
once before   the day I saw the Lady   the day my
life was changed.

I was seventeen   a sudden storm   I slipped into a
grove of trees I noticed certain things   the trees like
breaking waves above me   the piping of the birds
and then an eerie silence   I could hear the rain the
wind the birds but only at a distance   where I stood
there was no sound at all. Then I turned and saw
her   standing in the shelter of a tree   her dress as
golden as the sun   I felt that rush of terror then the
rising joy. She smiled and reached towards me
said Mircea   they questioned me forever on that
point and yet it's true   I swear on everything that's
holy she did call me by my name.

It was a shining moment in my life. How was I to
know there would be others   that one day I'd see
the shadows   she was just the first of many but I
didn't know that then   I spoke of her and everything was changed.

I think about what followed   all the men who sat
across from me at tables   asked me questions
wrote down every word I said   tried to confuse me
to convince me I'd imagined it   as if I could imagine it   then folded up their books said bless you
child and went away. What did they think I would
go back to being what I was   that people would
forget I'd ever seen her. It's not a thing that anyone
forgets.

That's why I never talk about these things   the
dream the shadows I see dancing on the cliffs   for
years I've seen them   I don't speak of them   not me
not anymore   I tell no one.

BEN: I just found the most amazing piece of wood. It was
              lying in the shadow of a rock, down towards the
              sea. Before I'd even picked it up, the shape inside
              assaulted me. A bull. A bull embedded in a piece of
              wood, struggling to break free.

              Not a placid creature, I can tell you that. A furious,
              glorious, terrible dark bull, a bull with testicles the
              size of melons. It's so real for me, so much alive
              already

              I can almost hear it bellow.

MIRCEA: In the village this afternoon I walked as always by
the men   all the old men with moustaches sitting
in the shade. They fell silent as they have since I
was seventeen but the last one in the row stuck out
his foot as I was passing by. I stumbled. They
laughed.

BEN: It isn't a bull, it's a minotaur! It struck me in the
              middle of the night. I'd made a few preliminary
              cuts but the wood felt cold, resistant. I found my-
              self unable to go on. And then

              I watched Mircea dressing in the moonlight,
              watched the liquid, languid movements of her na-
              ked arms, her legs. Watched her bend to pick her
              dress up from the floor

              And suddenly I saw the wood as it was meant to
              be: a man, rising from the body of a bull.

              My God, no wonder it's so furious. I sensed that
              fury from the start, I felt it in the wood: an awful
              unfulfilled and unfulfillable desire. What a crea-
              ture, when you think about it. What a concept! One
              being, locked forever in a battle with itself. What
              the bull in it desires, the man despises. What the
              man in it desires, the bull destroys. It can't be other-
              wise.

              I rose and moved across the room. Picked up the
              wood, and weighed it in my hands. Turned it in the
              moonlight, this way, that way. Picked up a knife,
              sat down. Put the wood between my knees. Began.

              The moon set, and the sun came up. I felt the heat
              grow sharper on my arms, my chest. I looked up,
              finally, and blinked. I hadn't dressed, or washed. I
              hadn't kissed Mircea when she left. I let her slip
              away without a word.

              But I have it now, I have it. It opened in my hands
              like a gift. From the waist up it's a man; below that
              it's a bull. It might be better if it weren't that way.
              Better for the minotaur, I mean.

MIRCEA: Which is finer I can't say   the part that's man the
part that's beast   I shuddered when he gave it to
me   whether out of fear or admiration I don't
know   I only know this work this minotaur
eclipses all the others in his face I read the truth he
knows it too.

I set it on the shelf beside my bed   at night when I
slip back from being with him it's this carving I
want near me   I can feel the struggle in it   all the
anger pride frustration   the war inside it raging
the reaching up to ecstasy   the stubborn down-
ward pull. There's terror there's euphoria   these
things go hand in hand   everywhere you see this
especially on Santorini   in the landscape in the
people if you know them well you sense it there's
a darkness trapped inside them that's at war   at
war with light.

BEN: Of course I'm like that too; I'm like the minotaur. On my way to the sea this morning I was thinking of the frescoes they've uncovered in the ancient city. How beautiful they are, as beautiful as anything a human being ever made. How prematurely modern: the purity of line, the elegance, simplicity, the rhythm

And suddenly I had to have her, had to have Mircea. The line of her back, the curve of her thigh, the arc of her breast: these things obsessed me.

I wrestled with myself. It was a little after nine. I couldn't turn around and simply show up at her door. Her mother, after all. The neighbours.

But I did just that. I climbed back up the hill, knocked once at her door, burst in. She was sitting at a table in a dressing gown. Her hair was loose around her. She seemed surprised, but not displeased. With a simple motion she undid her dressing gown.

I've never wanted anything so much in all my life. I'd have taken her, I think, with all the island watching. I'd have taken her no matter what the cost.

MIRCEA: This morning on my door a word   one word   and
            it wasn't madonna.

BEN: I've taken to walking around with a saw.

I need it now. I've picked the island clean of scraps of wood. Now I have to work for them.

There's a tree that grows near the sea, its trunk and limbs twisted by the wind into a wealth of haunting shapes. I study the shapes. I choose the one I like.

I found a beauty yesterday. Again the form I see here is a bull. A real bull, this time, not a thwarted one. A bull with all its power intact.

And as I carve, a flash of something that is not quite memory. Awareness? Recognition? I don't know, I only know

I love this animal I carve.

MIRCEA: She's had the village in not just the neighbours all
            the village   even children   led them to my room
               no one goes in there showed them all his carv-
            ings   let them touch them   let them giggle titter
            gawk. Why I asked her   why do such a thing   to
            witness my disgrace she says   disgrace disgrace
            disgrace.

BEN: Obscene, he calls them. Grabs me in the village square, this man I've never met, and calls my work obscene. Rants on and on about the Virgin Mary— I think that's what he said, his English wasn't very good, I think he said madonna—something about the madonna and then plenty more about my carvings, how I'd littered Santorini with bare breasts and massive testicles and penises the size of trees— the size of trees! It would be funny if it wasn't

And I haven't littered anything, I gave them to Mircea. All my carvings now I give

I swear I give them only to Mircea.

MIRCEA: This morning quite early the priest came uninvited
               knocked on the door before I'd even finished
               breakfast   it took me by surprise   I stood there
               staring couldn't seem to think   he said please ask
               me in Mircea   there are heads craned all up and
               down the street   we wouldn't want to cause an
               accident now would we. I took him to the kitchen
               gave him coffee and a little something   sat across
               from him   we talked of this and that. At last he said
               my child   I knew I was in trouble then   my child
               he called me then he sighed then he began. It pains
               me to go into this he said   then he went into it   he
               seemed to know so much   too much   went on
               forever   didn't miss a thing except a few good
               places where he might have stopped. I don't re-
               member everything   the tone of it and certain
               words   embarrassment   that one stays with me
               an embarrassment   that's what he told me I'd
               become.

               I didn't interrupt I let him finish   let the silence
               grow between us   well Mircea he said finally   I'm
               waiting. I touched the chain I wear around my neck
                   the crucifix I've worn since I was small   I want
               to spit on it   on it and everyone who's talked about
               me   I want to spit on all of them   I don't   I simply
               stand   and turn my back   and walk away.

BEN: When I came back to the village this afternoon I
                found her waiting for me by the market. This in
                itself was odd. But it wasn't that, it was the way she
                held herself—the shoulders squared, the head
                flung back, the body

                Perfectly composed. Mircea, what's the matter? I
                said—of course in English, as if that could possibly
                be any use. She shook her head and kissed me

                There, in front of half the village, she kissed me like
                she does when we're alone. Her breath was hot but
                when I touched her face the skin felt icy; I drew
                back in alarm. Are you sick, Mircea? But again she
                didn't understand. She took my hand and slipped
                it up beneath her blouse and placed it firmly on her
                breast. Still with people watching. I made a move
                to pull away but something stopped me, some

                Necessity I saw there, in her face. She smiled at me,
                then turned and cast a glance around her, at the
                sullen gaping people. A glance that shone with
                something

                Was it triumph? Or defiance.

                Mircea. Oh, Mircea.

                God help us both.

                (End of ACT ONE.)

ACT TWO

BEN: There's something going on here that I have to say I don't

Completely understand.

On Friday, when I stopped in the village for my mail, I felt a definite

Chill. An odd sensation, let me tell you—on such a white hot day. When I asked for my mail the clerk, Elina, the one who likes to flirt a little, handed it across with lowered eyes. Then quickly turned away. When I passed the kafenio, the men seated at the checkered tables, I felt their eyes following me. Not in a friendly way. Not with amusement, as they used to do, but with

Hostility. No, I'm not imagining this. I know I've offended these people.

Of course I've offended them. It's only a village, after all. We haven't been consistently discreet. Consistently? We haven't been discreet.

I think of all the times I lingered in her doorway. That afternoon outside the market. For weeks now she's been coming to me in my room at night. And it isn't enough to say it's late, it's dark, she slips through the streets like a shadow. We're adults, and the door is closed. It isn't enough, in a place like this. I know that

Now.

But I can't help thinking

It's not their sensibilities that I've offended—not just that. There's something else.

That man who stopped me in the village square, who called my work obscene. He puzzles me. Why should he care what I choose to carve? I don't display my carvings, sell them, hand them out to children. I give them to Mircea. Is that what he objects to, that I give them to Mircea? Maybe I've crossed a line, some line I didn't know was there. When I tried to ask Mircea what I'd done, if I'd done something

It was hopeless. She covered my mouth with kisses. Told me with her body what I'd done to do again. Again, again, again. What do you do with a woman like that?

You do it again.

MIRCEA: On Sundays now I make a point of sitting at my window as the village goes to church   I watch them walking past   their prayer books held above their eyes against the sun   their faces properly composed   they see me from the corners of their eyes   they don't let on. Later in the distance I can hear the chanting of the priest   the congregation chants in turn   the bells ring out and then the villagers come back   I sit where they will have to see me   sometimes with my breasts exposed   if I had snakes I'd hold them in my hands   hold them writhing in the air above me   smile an enigmatic smile   just like the goddess Pasiphae   the one Ben carved   I think I understand her now   I think I know exactly who she is.

My mother who's been far too ill for many days to rise up from her bed miraculously rises now comes hobbling to the window draws the curtains   panagea mou she whispers Holiest of Mothers have you lost your mind. I shrug   it was the fashion on these islands once upon a time   with any luck it may catch on again. She drifts away   too sad to speak   I open up the curtains but the street is empty   no one loiters in the doorways   no one stops to chat   no children play   not here not on this street   it's been like this every Sunday since I left the church.

BEN: This afternoon I found a note under my door. Not
              much of a note. Three words scrawled on a scrap of
              paper. In Latin, of all things. I suppose they knew I
              wouldn't understand the Greek.

              Corruptio optimi pessimus.

              I felt a little stunned. And then I realized: of course
              they meant Mircea. They think I've corrupted her.

              When she came at last I pulled her down beside me
              on the bed. Untied the ribbon she insists on wear-
              ing in her hair. Ran a finger all around her mouth.
              Took the scrap of paper from my pocket. Handed it
              to her.

MIRCEA: I don't know what it said exactly   I just knew this
was the moment we could turn away from silence
    if we did we'd lose each other   in a flash I saw
this   I saw it and I knew what I had to do.

BEN: She read it silently as I sat watching. She read it, and

She laughed.

MIRCEA: What would I have told him if I could have told
him about the dreams the visions the years of
adoration which I neither wanted nor deserved a
thousand prayers a thousand intercessions and for
what a people who now turn against me who
saw my rapture rising like a lark above them cast
their net into the skies to bring it down. For this I
can't forgive them after all the times they came to
me the pleas the supplications pray for me Mircea
  for my wife my child my lover I need I need I
have to have I want I want I want while I slept
alone and heard it through the open windows the
whining of the bedsprings the moans the sighs the
cries while I ached for it in all my being while my
arms I might have said this never have I said this
  my arms ached for the children I would never
hold.

BEN: I don't know; it doesn't sit easily with me. She can
          laugh about it—I'm glad to see her laugh.

          It doesn't sit easily. Every time I look at her, those
          words slide into view. Corruptio optimi pessimus.
          The corruption of the best is the worst.

          This morning very early while she slept, I lay
          awake. I watched her. She looked

          So fragile, lying there, one arm across her breast,
          the other flung out to the side. She looked like a
          doll some child had cast aside. I took her in my
          arms, I wanted

          To protect her, I suppose. But how? How can I
          protect her when the thing she needs protection
          from apparently

          Is me.

MIRCEA: I feel him watching me I feel   the questions rising
in his mind it worries me I know where questions
lead. I touch his face I draw him up and over to the
table sit him down   set a carving in his hands
stand behind him being careful not to touch him
will him to begin. At first he only stares at it unsee-
ing then he seems to recognize the weight of it the
shape the feel he turns it gently this way that way
    runs a finger all across it reaches for a knife
begins.

BEN: I try not to think about these things, I try

                To concentrate on carving. But even here, I seem to find

                More questions than answers. Why does every piece of wood I bring home now cry out to become a bull? I've carved half a dozen in the last few weeks. And why do I find them so beautiful? I don't mean my carvings; I mean bulls. I'll carve a thigh, and suddenly catch my breath. The line, the tension, the sleekness of the hide, the sense of power

                A power leashed, but barely, barely in control. These things I find so beautiful.

                This morning, as Mircea was leaving, I handed her another. I must admit I felt a little sheepish. I've given her so many bulls. Maybe it was my imagination, but I'd swear she took it from me just as though it were

                The perfect offering.

MIRCEA: Lately when I go from shop to shop there's never
            anything I need   the last one has always just been
            sold   at times the doors are locked   the people turn
            their backs. Sometimes on my doorstep there's a
            basket   some bread or fish a little fruit   there are
            still a few believers but they're frightened   they
            slip out in the dark of night   praying that they
            won't be seen. I want to hate them for it   but I can't.
            They wanted a madonna   their very own madonna
               someone who would intercede for them when
            all their own prayers failed   I didn't ask for it and
            yet I didn't stop it   didn't know a way to stop it   to
            deny them what they wanted to believe. Now of
            course they blame me   they think that I misled
            them   they feel betrayed abandoned   I suppose
            embarrassed   their madonna isn't a madonna after
            all but just a woman   just an ordinary woman
            what use is there in that.

BEN: There was never a woman more beautiful, not on
              earth, not on this earth; I'm convinced of it. No one
              ever had such eyes, such breasts, such hair. And
              the mouth, the mouth. This is a mouth imagined by
              a god. Inside

              Inside such heat, like lava, molten lava. When she
              spreads her legs to me, everything that ought to
              matter

              Slides away. In fact, it's only recently occurred to
              me to wonder

              Why she chose me over all the men on earth

              Well, anyway, on Santorini. The more I see of her,
              the more

              Remarkable it seems.

MIRCEA: Sometimes now when I arrive at Ben's I bare my
                 breasts I don't know why it feels right when I'm
                 with him   often I find him sitting with his head
                 bent low another carving I kiss him gently on the
                 neck to let him know I've come then open up my
                 dress and sit across from him he likes to glance up
                 from his work and see me there   my breasts ex-
                 posed my hair untied and falling loose my eyes on
                 him. From time to time he pauses in his work   he
                 reaches out to run his palm around my breasts
                 across my nipples moves a strand of hair behind
                 my shoulder touches my lips studies my face as
                 though it holds the answer to a question   some
                 desperate question   then sighs and wipes his
                 mouth and bends to his work again.

                 These for me are the best nights I watch him work
                     often he wears nothing but a pair of shorts   his
                 shoulders so elegant his skin so smooth the shape
                 of his head the curve of his arms his chest I long
                 to touch him but I don't I watch and wait. I know
                 that when he sets the wood aside at last we'll come
                 together like a kind of bursting   like a pent-up
                 mountain opening up into the sky.

BEN: The gods have been at work again.

              This morning, very early, I came suddenly awake.
              Mircea had just left; the sheets where she'd been
              lying were still warm. I understood at once where
              she had gone. I understood I had to follow her.

              As soon as I stepped into the street, I could see her
              up ahead, moving swiftly along the road that leads
              up to the cliffs. I followed at a distance, feeling
              sheepish yet compelled

              Compelled to follow. When she reached the sum-
              mit, I hung back amongst the rocks. There's no

              There's simply no explaining what I saw. There
              was a kind of

              Light, pulsating all around her. Her face took on a
              look

              Of rapture, joy, abandon. She bared her breasts to
              the moon, raised her arms toward the stars, and
              danced

              A violent, ecstatic dance.

              It sent a shiver through me.

MIRCEA: I can't explain it   something happened   the shad-
             ows took on form   their numbers stretched into
             infinity   the light so strong like daylight like the
             light around the Lady when I saw her   and I
             danced   I didn't mean to but they gathered round
             me   pulled me with them to the centre of the light
                they danced and I danced with them it was

             Like the first time I was with him with my Ben like
             that and all the other times together   I thought I'd
             die of rapture   thought I'd died.

BEN: I watched her dancing in that strange pulsating
                light

                My feelings in a turmoil. I wanted to race across
                and pull her back from the edge of the cliff, I
                wanted

                To join her in the dance. Strip off my clothes, raise
                my arms to the moon and writhe like a snake to the
                same soundless tune. I wanted to, I wanted to

                I couldn't do it.

                I turned, and slipped away.

MIRCEA: In time the dancing slowed the cliffs dissolved I
               saw a gentle rolling field   the shadows turned
               towards the field then back to me   they gestured
               with their arms for me to follow   I wanted to I
               wanted to   I couldn't do it. They didn't wait for
               long   they slipped away without a backward
               glance   left me standing in the fading light alone.

BEN: All the way home, I found I could think of nothing

              But the dance. What it was, and where she'd
              learned it. Why I felt as though I'd watched the
              dance before, in some

              In some

MIRCEA: Tonight as I sat reading to my mother reading her
to sleep as always she suddenly sat forward laid
her withered hand across my arm begged me in
the name of God the Father Christ the Saviour and
the Virgin Mother begged me in the name of all
that's holy end this madness now. I laid the book
aside then paused I couldn't find the words to say
and when I did I realized I didn't want to say them
          didn't want to hurt her mother I was never a
madonna this is what I should have said it would
have been the truth it would have killed her. There
was nothing I could do I raised her hand up to my
lips and kissed it   then set it gently down. She
sighed and leaned back on the pillow even such a
little effort wears her out she looked so frail so sad
so frightened   it took everything I had to walk
away.

BEN: I've done a terrible thing. I suppose you'd call it
                break and enter only

                There was nothing to break.

                I let myself into her house. Not only her house, her
                bedroom. I did. Just now. I didn't plan it, I just
                happened to see her leave. There was no one in the
                street. I tried the door, it wasn't locked. I slipped
                inside.

                It only took a second or two, to find her room. I saw
                a narrow bed, neatly made. A crucifix above it. A
                table with a lamp. A mat beside the bed. A shelf
                running all along one wall, holding all my little ill-
                formed animals, my birds and fish. The goddess
                Pasiphae, the tortured minotaur. And every-
                where—in every nook and cranny, on the window-
                sill, across the floor, the table, there were

                Bulls running, bulls leaping, bulls with their heads
                back, bellowing at the skies. In that room, in that
                narrow pristine space

                They set up a clamour that made the walls vibrate.
                And suddenly my mind

                Exploded with images. Of women in long flowing
                gowns, their beautiful breasts bare, walking
                amongst antelope and swallows and lilies. Of men
                setting off on voyages in elegant ships, escorted
                out to sea by schools of leaping dolphins. Of a
                world, a world

                A world of such simplicity, such purity, serenity

                Shattered, blown to pieces, in the time-span of a
                sigh.

MIRCEA: This morning very early coming back from Ben's I
         ran into a group of men not far from the taverna
         they had formed a circle in the centre of the circle
         one was dancing it was young Stephanos I've
         known him since he was a child in the pale light of
         the moon he danced as dark and fluid as a dream. I
         knew I shouldn't stop I couldn't help it there was
         something in this boy the way he moved   as
         though torn between heaven and earth as though
         uncertain whether to fly up or to fall down. I
         slipped into a doorway   stood as silent as a stone
         not moving hardly breathing wanting only to ob-
         serve the dance and then to slip away. Stephanos
         danced the moonlight deepened I realized they'd
         seen me a signal passed between them and a bottle
         too I slipped out of the doorway someone stepped
         in front of me   I turned to run the other way an-
         other man stepped forward   in the flutter of a
         heartbeat they had formed a circle round me like
         the circle round Stephanos who now danced alone.

         I knew these men and yet I didn't their faces dark
         their voices low their eyes like slits they called me
         whore. The circle they had formed grew tighter I
         felt a hand go up between my legs another on my
         breast whore I heard again and whore and whore
         and whore. One of them Mattheos leaned in close
         then spat she's come from him just now he said
         you can smell it on her you can smell it   then
         someone else moved in behind I felt his arms go
         round me heard my dress rip open heard a shout
         go up and then an awful silence they were ready
         for it but they were afraid. I didn't try to cover up I
         looked them in the eye looked each one in the eye
            I didn't speak until I knew they wouldn't miss a
         word. There isn't one of you who didn't come to
         me when I was your madonna now you want a
         different kind of service well it's yours I give it to
         you but you have to pray for it you have to get
         down in the dust the dirt and pray for me the way
         you've had me pray for you.

For a moment no one moved   I saw a hand go up
to wipe a mouth   a few heads turned away   they
were sober now they felt ashamed   Mattheos most
of all. When he spoke at last his voice was harsh
his words dropped down onto the street like stones
      the Xeni he said   the foreigners   they get it all.
Then he turned and walked away   the others
drifted off   I shivered   felt my knees give out   I
slumped down in the street   when I turned towards Stephanos he was gone.

BEN: When I woke this morning, it lay across me like a
sheet: knowledge. Certain knowledge.

I know who she is, now. I know.

I've been in a daze, I think—a drunken stupor.
Only without the benefit of drink.

My God.

My God, my God. My God.

MIRCEA: Last night when I arrived he was waiting for me
               hot and anxious   walked straight to me   wove his
               fingers through my hair and fanned it out around
               me   undid whatever buttons he could bother with
                   his need of me so great his hands his lips were
               everywhere at once. There was a fever an intensity
               and afterwards he wouldn't let me pull the sheet
               across my body   had to see me in the moonlight
               had to see me everywhere   he turned me like a
               carving this way that way   touched me with his
               eyes his hands   a line of concentration on his brow
               his face so serious as though he had to memorize it
               all. In time

               I fell asleep   and woke to find him leaning on his
               side still watching me. Mircea that was all he said
               and then his body heaved with sobs   dry sobs no
               tears   I found this so much worse than tears   it
               shattered me his pain   I reached for him I held him
               close we sobbed   together.

BEN: This morning, as I was shaving

There was a knock at my door. I opened it, and standing in the hallway were three men: the priest, an ancient man I didn't know and one of the local fishermen. Evangelos, I think he's called.

I asked them in. I offered each of them my only chair but each declined in turn and so we stood, the four of us, between the table and the bed. Two things were clear at once. Evangelos had been coerced; he had no wish to be there. The old man, on the other hand

Had plainly volunteered.

The priest spoke English. It's for Mircea that we've come, he said. Because we love her.

Yes, I said. Go on.

She was pure as rain from heaven, the old man blurted out. Until you came along.

Nikos, said the priest, be quiet. Let me deal with this. Then he turned to me. Nikos was the best friend of Mircea's father. He takes a father's interest. I'm sure you understand.

I nodded, only to encourage him.

In this country, he said, we have a saying: Better an old sandal with holes than a new one. You understand the meaning?

No, I said.

The priest was deeply disappointed, judging by his sigh. What it means, is this: it's better to marry a Greek than a foreigner.

Ah. I see.

Of course, this is an ancient saying, and we are a modern people. Because of this, the priest went on, and because of the esteem in which we hold

Mircea, we would probe our hearts for understanding, and having found it through the grace of God, I'm here to tell you we would not refuse to marry our Mircea. We would not refuse to marry her to you.

For a moment I was too

Astounded to respond. I thought of the three of them, conspiring together. No, it wouldn't be the three of them; it would be the priest and Nikos. I thought of them plotting their strategy. And suddenly—I don't know what came over me

I laughed. I leaned back on my heels and shook with laughter

At the absurdity of it all. Don't they know what they're suggesting? Have they no idea

Who she is?

At once, the room erupted into noise, confusion. Nikos waved his arms in all directions, bellowing at the priest, at me. The priest did his best to try and calm him. Evangelos wiped his cap across his thigh, and put it on, and left. The door slammed shut behind him.

Suddenly the other two fell silent. They glanced at the door, at me. The old man took a step in my direction, made the motion of a spit, then turned and shambled out.

I faced the priest. Suddenly it wasn't funny anymore. I wanted to apologize, I wanted to explain. But when I tried to speak, he raised his hands and turned his head aside. I am not your confessor, he said. Then he, too, turned and left.

I stood unblinking, staring at the door. My heart was thick with pain. In my ears a sound, a sound I recognized, a sound that shook me to the core. It was the sound of my illusions

Shattering.

MIRCEA: I see them coming out   I see Evangelos his face
dark with shame   then Nikos looking very pleased
and then at last the priest. I know at once that
they've conspired against me   all of them
Evangelos as well. I want to shout I want to raise
my voice up to the rooftops shout them down   I
can't I feel my mouth fill up with fear my heart
constrict   they've done it now   they've done it.

BEN: They're right, of course; they're absolutely right.

                  They came thinking they would shame me. Not
                  into marriage; that, I'm sure, was just a ruse. It's not
                  that they think I should marry her

                  They think I should leave.

                  And the worst of it is

                  I should.

MIRCEA: It's changing. I can hardly bear to say it but it's true
tonight for instance when I smiled at him he
glanced away   there was an awkwardness between us   where once there was a sense of time
expanding all around us when we came together
now it's time contracting   every moment precious
every touch defined   nothing squandered not a
glance a kiss a sigh   no accidents no carelessness
no waste.

BEN: In the mail today, three letters, three

Clanging reminders. Is this a coincidence, I wonder? Or do I blame the gods?

MIRCEA: The letters lie there on his table   right there on the
            table   letters in a feminine hand   tonight while he's
            asleep I slip across the room   I pick them up. He
            hasn't opened them but still he keeps them   as
            though he doesn't want to open up to her and yet
            can't bring himself to let her go.

            I turn towards him lying naked in the bed   she
            must be beautiful I think   perhaps like me her hair
            is long perhaps that's why he reaches for it first   I
            feel a rush of something then a stabbing pain. So
            this is it I whisper   this is what they mean by
            jealousy   I never dreamt it felt like this   so horrible
            so ugly so profound.

            I sink into the chair   I force myself to look at him   I
            know I have to think of everything   how he would
            touch her kiss her mount her   cry her name out in
            the wildest moments   but I don't know her name
            or who she is or if he loves her still   I don't know
            any of these things   how could I know.

BEN: This morning I went down to the sea to talk to
Evangelos. Why him, I couldn't say. Perhaps because he seemed so kind.

It was just past dawn. He and another man were
unloading the night's catch. Their wives stood
nearby, lifting and untangling and refolding the
nets. All along the beach, the scene was repeated:
men pouring the fish into baskets, to be mounted
on donkeys and motorbikes; women in their simple dresses clearing the yellow nets. The air was
fresh, the sea lapped against the shore, the light
was golden from the newly-risen sun. I watched at
a distance, partly hidden by a cluster of rocks.

Finally Evangelos led his donkey with its sagging
baskets away from the boat and up the beach towards me. I waited until he drew quite close, then
stepped into his path. He seemed startled, but not
angry. With a gesture of his head, he motioned me
to join him.

As soon as we had turned onto the road that leads
to Akrotiri, I wished I hadn't come. What did I
expect to accomplish? Did I think I could explain
myself? There was no explaining what I had to do.

Evangelos seemed to sense my discomfort. He
tossed his cigarette away. We have a saying here,
he said.

Yes, I know you do.

He grinned. No, this is another one. Listen, here on
Santorini we say of ourselves: we're not people,
we're Santorinians. Why do we say this? Because
we live on the edge of the precipice. The land trem-
bles underneath us; we're used to this. From time
to time in the caldera the mountain grows restless;
this we're used to, too. We live here in defiance of
the gods. We dare them to shake us down.

But there's a price, he said. Of course there's a price
to pay

For such defiance. We pay it. We go on.

I turned towards him. I was on the verge of saying what I'd come to say, but again he seemed to sense it. He raised his hand.

Mircea, he said, finally

Is Santorinian. She knows what it means to live on the precipice. Do you see what I'm telling you? She knows.

I felt my heart catch, felt my feet stop moving. He touched his fingers to his cap in a kind of salute, barked an order to the donkey, and moved on.

I watched until he disappeared around a bend, feeling

Emptier, and more alone

Than I had felt when I first came here. I turned toward the sea; it glimmered in the distance like a sheet of burnished metal. Somewhere a rooster crowed. The air was heavy with oregano. Farther up the road, around another bend, someone revved an engine. Already the day was growing hot.

It will be like this, I thought, two days from now. It will all be here

Like this

But I'll be gone.

MIRCEA: This afternoon I see him walking in the village   see
               him for the first time as the others see him I sup-
               pose   an ordinary man   a stranger with a secret
               past   a foreigner   one of the many foreigners who
               come and gawk   take what they like from the is-
               land   go away. I know then it can happen   he can
               leave me on a moment's notice   I will go some
               evening to his room and find it empty   nothing left
               of him except a hair curled in the bedsheets   even
               Minos   poor misshapen Minos   will be gone.

BEN: She hasn't come.

              She hasn't come the last two nights, and I can't
              leave without

              Without

MIRCEA: This morning Sostis The Man of the Volcano took
                 me across the caldera to Thirasia   took me reluc-
                 tantly the wind was up the boat rocked eerily from
                 side to side   he was afraid to dock   I had to leap
                 into the sulky water   wade ashore. He watched me
                 from the boat until he knew that I was safe   then
                 waved and turned for home.

                 I climbed the cliff   sat for hours looking back across
                 the sea at Santorini   at my life   my past that's like
                 a distant country   whose border now is closed.

                 In the afternoon I found it   a chapel I remembered
                      the ancient lonely chapel of Saint Irene. I slipped
                 inside   the air was cool   I sat there quietly alone. It
                 was a sign I wanted I suppose   some sign to guide
                 me   peace of mind to settle on me   nothing hap-
                 pened   nothing came. I rose to leave   that's when I
                 saw it   the baptismal font   I knelt beside it   caught
                 my breath. It was carved with bulls and garlands
                 prancing bulls entrancing garlands   bulls who
                 wore their horns like crowns weaving in and out of
                 garlands   you could sense the rapture the abandon
                 in that dance of flesh and flower   you could see it
                 almost smell it   that shameless celebration   not of
                 lust exactly but of life. I've had that   this is what I
                 told myself   I've had it and I'm glad I've had it
                 glad I had the chance to choose it   but what do I
                 choose now.

                 I turned away at last   stepped from the coolness of
                 the chapel into the hot bright air   on the doorstep
                 sat an old woman dressed all in black   at her side a
                 basket   she reached into the basket drew out a
                 tomato   a luscious red tomato   offered it to me.
                 Once you've had a taste she said you never get
                 enough   then she smiled a toothless smile and
                 turned away.

BEN: I've been to see the priest.

He didn't particularly want to let me in, I could see that on his face, but he was too polite to turn me away. He ushered me into a little room behind the altar. We sat across from one another on a pair of wooden chairs, our knees almost touching. Without his robes, he didn't look at all the way he had the other day. He looked quite frail. He waited for me to speak.

I owe you an apology, I said. For my behaviour.

He didn't say a word. He waited.

I'd like to do right by Mircea, but I don't know if I can. There are

Complications. I really think it would be better if I

If

Still the priest was silent. He brushed a fleck of something from his knee.

I swallowed hard. The room was warm. In the distance I could hear a donkey bray. A truck labouring up a hill. A mother calling to a child, the child's reply. At that moment, in that tiny room, on that island where the worst has happened, I saw my life for what it was: a sorry little rag of a thing.

Father, I know the price of joy. I know the price!

When I'm with Mircea—you may find this shocking, but I don't know any other way to say it— when I'm with Mircea

God walks burning through us. Burning! And I can't do it, I don't think that I can

Bring myself to do it. I can't let that wither away into

Conventionality, into

Banality, into

Conversation! Into, into

The priest sighed deeply. When I glanced at him, I
realized the sigh came not from disappointment
but compassion.

I dropped my head into my hands.

Father, do you think it's possible—remotely possible

That a man who wasn't born on Santorini could

Could somehow

I felt his hand fall gently on my shoulder.

When I raised my head again, the room was empty.
Even the day had gone.

MIRCEA: When Sostis comes for me at last it's very late   the wind is high and fretful   he pulls the boat in close he shakes his head. Look at you he shouts   you're quite a picture. I suppose I am   a woman all in white sitting on a rock beside the glowering sea holding in her lap a red tomato.

I climb into the boat   Sostis wraps a blanket round me   we set out across the sea for Santorini   the boat pitching violently the seaspray lashing over us   I don't look up I keep my head down all the way across   my eyes glued to the tomato. I think about the woman all in black   her words to me   once you've had a taste she said you never get enough   I think of Ben   my nights with him   the shadows and the night I danced with them

And suddenly I have it   in that heaving sea-swept boat it comes to me   I know what I have to do.

BEN: I spend the evening

Wandering the island. I don't see anything; that is, I don't remember anything I see. It seems to me a storm is building. The wind hammers at my ears. Eventually I find myself

Standing in Mircea's darkened doorway. I knock, but no one answers. The windows are completely shuttered.

I drift back to my room, I sit at the table and I write

The longest letter of my life. It's hard to do—my God, it's hard to do—but it feels good to have it done. It feels as though I've finally shut a door.

When it's finished I go out again, and mail it. Come back home.

Wait for Mircea.

MIRCEA: We dock at last   I stumble from the boat   my
               clothes my hair are drenched with sea   Sostis
               drives me home   high above us in the village the
               wires twist and whine   the sky heaves with thun-
               der.

BEN: In the middle of the night it comes to me—what I
                have to do. I have to take her away. Not forever;
                God no, not forever. For a while. Just until we get to
                know each other

                In a different way.

                I haven't slept a wink and now I pace between the
                table and the bed—the bed, the table—feeling

                Giddy with excitement. I'll get the priest to trans-
                late! I'll ask her to go back with me—to Canada!

MIRCEA: I dream that dream I never could remember until now I dream of great dark birds in flight their wings spread wide to catch the wind their white cheeks gleaming in the sun I see them flying two by two these birds these wise impassioned birds who mate for life.

BEN: I want to take you there, I'll say—to Canada. We'll
              fly away together. In a plane, she'll ask. I'll laugh.
              Who needs a plane? We'll spread our wings and
              fly away, like geese, like Canada geese. They mate
              for life, Mircea, did you know?

MIRCEA: I dress quickly steal out quietly then run along the road that leads up to the cliffs   the sea is black and angry the wind tears at my clothes   but they are there where I have always seen them   dancing in a ring of shifting light   they turn towards me they embrace me   draw me with them to the centre of the light   I raise my arms to dance

And suddenly my arms aren't arms at all but wings great wings   I'm lifting diving spinning circling circling like a bird towards the future towards

BEN: Light. A strange pulsating light, and then a burst of
                rapture. Don't ask me how I know; I do. I see the
                cliffs dissolve and then

                And then

                I run through Akrotiri, pounding on doors. I rouse
                half the village but no one understands me, no one

                Understands! Finally Evangelos appears. We
                climb into his ancient pickup and the two of us race
                along the road that leads up to the cliffs. It's slick
                with rain, that road. The wind howls like a living
                thing, diabolical. Finally we reach the top. We leap
                from the truck

                But of course she isn't there, why would she

                Be there?

                (A long silence.)

BEN: At the service, the priest embraced me. So did
Evangelos. We'll find her body yet, he said. We'll
find it.

I let it go. I'm touched by their compassion, their
determination

To bend this loss into a shape they know.

BEN: I still dream of it—my island washed in light. But
              now

              I'm standing where the mountain used to stand—
              in the heart of the caldera—in the instant just be-
              fore the sea pours in. Around me the walls of the
              caldera soar up towards a wide blue ragged

              Swatch of sky. I know the sea is poised there, be-
              neath that swatch of sky. I see the first drop fall,
              and then the second. The trickle turns into a
              stream, into a flood, into a massive waterfall, a wild
              ferocious plunging

              Thundering waterfall. I want to say a word

              One word, before the water hits me. I seem to know
              the word I want to say. I open my mouth but in that
              very instant

              The sea pours in.

              The word is washed away.

              Strange. It's not the terror of the sea that wakes me.
              It's the sorrow for that lost unspoken word.

BEN: I find it very difficult

To carve. I try, but the wood resists me. I set it aside. I turn towards the window but there's nothing there: a pale rectangle in a wooden frame.

I stretch out on the bed and try to sleep. I realize I haven't anything—nothing at all that once belonged to her. A comb, a photograph, a ribbon. A lock of her hair. Her hair! I close my eyes and try to remember the weight of it, the scent, the sheen. Gone.

The wind dies down. The sea darkens into oil. I drift into a fitful sleep

And wake to find her standing in the doorway, dressed all in white like a bride, her hair loose and wild and tangled, in her hand a ripe tomato. She looks like a vision from another world, a world

As yet unborn.

I thought you'd never come, I say. I've missed you. She understands, I know she understands, and yet she doesn't move; she stands there staring at me, on her face a look I've never seen. God, Mircea, don't do this to me. Don't keep yourself away.

She runs across the room. I move to kiss her, move to kiss her

And she's gone, I'm kissing

Air.

(Silence.)

BEN: More than ever, as the months go by

I draw comfort from the people of Atlantis. I feel such kinship with them, such nostalgia for them, all those people moving in that dawn-like world. I wonder

Whether what once was and is no more is truly lost to us—lost forever as we've come to think—or whether we reclaim it in some way

If only in our dreams, our longings. Maybe the past isn't a place we leave behind, but a place we circle

Towards.

It's possible. I believe it's possible.

And sometimes when the moon is full, I find myself moving in the dead of night along the road that winds up to the cliffs. I move as though pulled by an invisible string, and when I get there, I strip to the skin, raise my arms to the moon and writhe like a snake to my own

Soundless tune. I don't see anything, but sometimes, sometimes when the sea is wild, I imagine that I writhe

In light.

The End